The Great Book of the Fantastic Creatures of Atlantis

Text by Giuseppe D'Anna

Illustrations by Anna Láng

Contents

INTRODUCTION 4

SHALLOW WATER CREATURES 6

    Mermaid 8

    Zaratan 12

    Hippocampus 16

    Akhlut 20

    Makara 24

    Aughisky 26

    Capricornus 28

CREATURES OF THE ABYSS 30

    Kraken 32

    Umibozu 36

    Cadborosaurus 40

    Namazu 44

    Cecaelia 48

    Adaro 50

    Isonade 52

    Cirein-Cròin 54

A BRIEF GUIDE TO SEA CREATURES 56

    The Five Golden Rules of the Sea 57

    Bluer than Blue: Keep the Sea Clean, It's a Sea Creature's Home 58

    At the Bottom of the Sea: The Atlantis Legend 60

    Final Test to Become a Sea Creature Guardian 62

Introduction

Hiya!

My name is Karen. Are you ready to dive in?

Before you do, you'll need flippers, a mouthpiece, and a dive mask, because we're about to set off for the deep blue abyss!

No, we're not going treasure hunting (although that's not to say we won't find any); we're actually off on a voyage of discovery to find out about the many fantastic creatures that live in the sea!

You might not be aware, but there are hundreds of weird and wonderful animals hiding below the surface. I'm not talking about anchovies, octopus, and tuna either, though I'll admit they're special. No, I'm thinking more about wonderful mermaids, giant Zaratan, bizarre-looking Umibozu. . . .

Follow me and you'll learn how to recognize (and to find) each of them—only watch out, or they may find you!

Trust me, I might look like an ordinary girl, but I'm actually an expert—or, to be more precise, a qualified Sea Creature Guardian!

How did I become one? That's easy: I traveled far and wide exploring the seven seas and studied every creature I encountered.

It all came about by chance, when a hippocampus (you'll find out what that is if you read on!) saved me from the waves of a stormy sea and carried me to the shore. What an incredible day that was!

After that, I decided to set sail to visit our planet's many seas and oceans: I wanted to find that hippocampus and thank it in person. To my surprise, I met many more creatures along the way, each more extraordinary than the next.

I kept notes about everything I learned, and I wrote them all in this notebook. But please be careful. It's a treasure trove of information, touching on some of the darkest mysteries of the sea. Use it wisely!

At the end, you'll have to take the official test. Why? To become an official Sea Creature Guardian! Once you've finished reading my notes, you can give it a try. But don't worry, I'll explain it all later, a bit at a time.

So, what do you say?

Are you coming diving with me?

Take a deep breath.

Hold your nose. . . .

SPLASH!

Shallow Water Creatures

I'll admit, I started my notebook talking about the abyss (we will get there, honest!); but I think an exploration of some of the creatures living just under the surface is a better place to start.

Firstly, because they're the easiest to meet . . . if you know where to look!

Don't be fooled, though. They occasionally get close to the shore and may even approach humans like you and me, but that doesn't mean they're any less dangerous.

Get on the wrong side of a mermaid, for example, maybe by ruffling her hair, or walk a little too close to a Capricornus and its rock-hard horns, and you'll remember the experience for a long time.

I'm not kidding. So keep your eyes peeled, okay?

But there's no need to be afraid: if you follow my advice (and don't ruffle a mermaid's hair), you'll be just fine.

Mermaid
Classification: Human-Fish Hybrid

All sailors claim to have seen at least one during their time at sea—a woman with long, beautiful hair; a sweet, lilting voice; and a tail covered in glittering scales. Mermaids are half-woman, half-fish, and undoubtedly among the most famous creatures of the sea.

You may see one sitting on the rocks by the shore sometime, maybe admiring herself in a mirror (where did she get it? Try to be patient: the secrets of her many trinkets will soon be revealed to you as well!), or she could appear at sea to passing ships, with a smile for the crews. Mermaids are not the slightest bit shy; but be careful: a formidable character lies behind her pretty face, and if they ever feel that they've been insulted (it doesn't take much, as they're quite touchy), they'll take immediate revenge, luring ships straight onto submerged ridges.

This is why ancient ships used to have a figurehead (the wooden ornament that decorated the bow) in the shape of a mermaid: the crew hoped such a vain creature would never sink a ship with her own face on the front! What a clever idea!

The large fin helps her move around quickly. With a quick flick, she can disappear into the deep blue sea.

Mermaids don't wear clips in their hair (the water would ruin them): they use shells and starfishes instead.

A mermaid's tail has many colors: red, blue, green. . . .

Favorite Pastimes:

Mermaids are fascinated with objects from the human world and are often tempted to approach humans to get their hands on one. They're such incurable collectors! If something precious falls from a ship into the sea, they scoop it up and take it straight back to their cave, to be hoarded with all the other treasures they've come across.

But don't be too anxious to give chase! You could be sorely disappointed—because while all mermaids think everything shiny is valuable, it may just be a boring old fork to you!

What to do When you Meet a Mermaid

Put your fingers in your ears right away (or wear earphones and turn your favorite music up loud), because a mermaid's most lethal weapon is her spellbinding song, which she uses to attract ships and then make them sink!

Christopher Columbus also wrote in his diaries that he'd seen a mermaid.

There's a mermaid with the tail of a salmon in the sea off Scotland, and it's said that she would grant three wishes for her release if she is ever captured (although I'd think twice about getting tangled up with her in the first place!).

The male equivalent to a mermaid is a Triton (not a merman!).

Zaratan
Classification: Giant Cetacean

Imagine that you've sailed to a mysterious island. Have you landed? Well, now imagine that the island starts to move. Worse than that, it's sinking. The stuff of nightmares. Yet this is exactly what happens when you meet a Zaratan (and no, not in a dream!).

It might be hard to believe, but this gigantic creature is often disguised as an island. Yes, really, an island! But I don't think it does it on purpose. The problem is that when it rises to the surface to bask in the sunshine, it often dozes off. Then, before you know it, trees, forests, hills, even small villages spring up on its back!

Zaratans look similar to a whale—only much, much bigger.

When the Zaratan realizes this, it dives back under water for a good old scrub! You can't blame it, either. How would you like to have hordes of tiny insects crawling on your back?

Favorite Pastimes:

In truth, Zaratans only rise to the surface for some peaceful shut-eye, although with all those comings and goings on its back, that can't be easy!

Luckily, Zaratans are not light sleepers. But be careful! If even one campfire is lit on the "island," the fright will have it diving back under the water before you know it!

What to do When you Meet a Zaratan

You might not realize you're looking at one until it suddenly wakes up. At that point, you'll have only a few seconds to snatch a quick peek before it disappears back into the sea (it will normally announce that it's awake with a flap of its flippers and a spurt of water).

If you end up on top of one, you probably won't see anything (when it wakes up, I mean). You'll merely be in a forest one minute, and then floating in the sea the next!

Another (very complicated) name for a Zaratan is aspidochelone.

Zaratans have often been described as giant turtles rather than whales. Maybe there are two different kinds!

Hippocampus
Classification: Horse-Fish Hybrid

Lots of my friends love ponies, but I'd much rather ride a hippocampus any day!

Hippocampi (often called sea horses) are half-horse, half-fish, and are the loyal steeds of mermaids and tritons, the only ones able to mount them. They grab onto the animal's neck and wrap their tails around the hippocampus's tail.

There are numerous stories of how Poseidon, god of the sea according to the Greeks, drove a chariot drawn by beautiful hippocampi through the seven seas.

Hippocampi are obviously sea creatures, but don't forget that indomitable spirit of a horse. If you force a hippocampus to stop, it will snort and kick until you let it go again (admit it, you do the same when you're bored!).

What do hippocampi love most? To roam freely in the ocean depths, past coral reefs and shoals of fish. And yes, they spray sea foam everywhere, but what a lot of fun they have doing it!

Watch out for the tail: like horses, they whip them fast!

Favorite Pastimes:

The best thing in the world for a hippocampus is to be able to move like the wind (yes, I know I've said it before, but it's very important). They especially like swimming near beaches and along the coast.

When I was young, and by that I mean very young, my mom and dad would often stop me from going into the sea because of the "white horses." Now I get it! They were referring to hippocampi racing about at crazy speeds, whipping up enormous waves and causing them to break into white foam on the shore, which can be terrifying!

What to do When you Meet a Hippocampus

Don't try to mount it; there'd be no point! It might look like a horse, but its skin is as slippery as a fish's.

The word *hippocampus* also means some other things, like an ordinary seahorse or even part of our brain (yes, right there in our head).

Hippocampi are featured in numerous fountains. Take a good look the next time you come across one.

Akhlut
Classification: Wolf-Orca Hybrid

This creature of the Arctic Ocean is as striking as it is dangerous (so be extremely careful!).

Half-orca, half-wolf, they are fast-moving, silent predators, both on land and in the water.

Akhluts prefer the shadows of the abyss; but when they're hungry (which is often!), they come in to the coast to hunt for food, which means you have a good chance of seeing one near the surface.

If you do, I wouldn't recommend going over to pet it—not if you care about keeping your hand, that is!

Akhlut footprints are similar to a large wolf's. If you ever see any prints in the snow, you can recognize them easily because they always end in the sea!

But take heed. If the footprints are fresh, then the Akhlut is probably still around, lying in wait just below the surface of the water, for its next prey.

Yes, you're right, I find it frightening, too. It sends shivers running down the spine . . . not just from the cold!

An akhlut's coat dries right away, as soon as it comes out of the water.

An Akhlut's feet never slip on ice or wet rocks.

Favorite Pastimes:

Akhluts like to hunt at night. With their wolf eyes, they can see easily in the dark (whether it's at the bottom of the sea or in the depths of the forest).

Their black coat is easy to spot in the daytime, as it stands out against the white snow. Much safer for them to stay in the dark, hiding in the shadows and then jumping out at you when you least expect it!

What to do When you Meet an Akhlut

Don't run away immediately; there's a risk that it might follow you (and beware, it moves fast!).

Retreat quietly and leave it to its hunting. If it does come after you, climb a tree. You'll be safe up there. Akhluts are too fast to be outrun or outswum; but when it comes to climbing, they're absolutely useless!

Makara

Classification: Friendly Hybrid

The name translates literally as *water monster*, and that's exactly what it is.

With an elephant's trunk, crocodile scales, and a fish tail, it's a real animal mishmash!

Not to mention the long, sharp teeth. Their teeth are particularly unpleasant, especially when they're up close to your face!

Appearances can be deceiving, though. Makaras are actually quite meek and friendly to anyone they meet.

An Indian sailor once told me that they even bring good luck and ward off evil spirits, which is why they're often painted on the doors and columns of palaces. In these pictures, the makara is shown with a lotus flower or a shiny pearl in its jaws, both symbols of good fortune and prosperity.

The scales all over their bodies are as hard as stone and as smooth as ice.

Makaras are meek, but I still wouldn't upset them. If the claws ever come out, be very careful!

Aughisky

Classification: Horse-Fish Hybrid

Don't be taken in by an Aughisky's looks (yes: this time, appearances are definitely deceiving!).

It might look like a magnificent black horse, but it's actually a very dangerous sea creature.

The Aughisky usually trots from beach to beach, appearing kind and good-natured enough to persuade unsuspecting passersby to climb on. That's when it reveals its true nature, taking off at full speed for the sea, dragging its poor victim in with it.

Don't fall for it, okay? Keep away.

And be careful about the people around you. The Aughisky can also shapeshift into a human to hoodwink you! Luckily, when it does transform, it always seems to forget a minor detail, like its horses' hooves or seaweed in its hair. So keep your eyes peeled and it won't fool you!

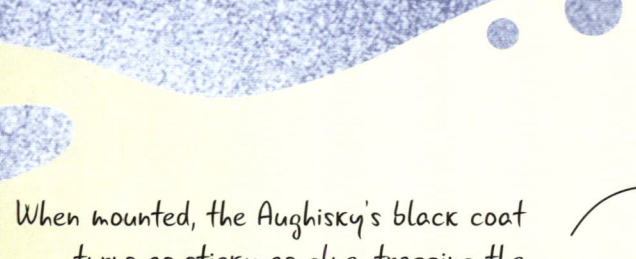

When mounted, the Aughisky's black coat turns as sticky as glue, trapping the unlucky rider who can't get away.

Capricornus
Classification: Goat-Fish Hybrid

Anyone who uses the expression "as stubborn as a mule" has evidently never met a Capricornus. The only things more unbending than this creature are its horns....

Even though the fish part of its body needs to be in the water, the goat half is so obstinate that it will keep scrambling up cliffs, digging its hooves in, and often attempting to climb the very steepest rock faces at the edge of the sea!

In other words, Capricornus keeps going up and up until its fish half forces it to go back to the water. It's a hard life!

Yet this legendary bullheadedness has made it so famous that there's a constellation of stars with the same name, *Capricorn*. It's even one of the twelve signs of the zodiac!

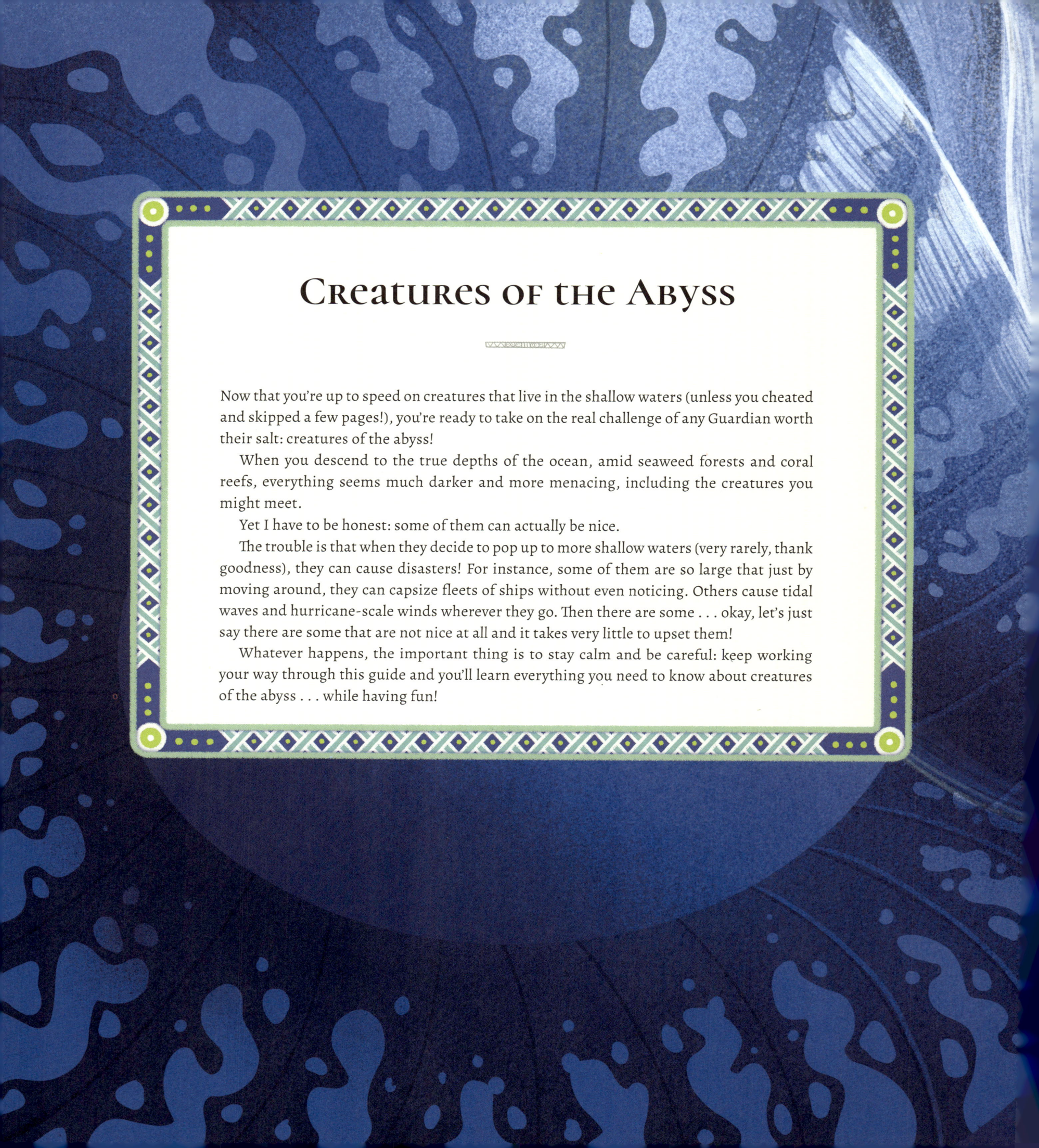

Creatures of the Abyss

Now that you're up to speed on creatures that live in the shallow waters (unless you cheated and skipped a few pages!), you're ready to take on the real challenge of any Guardian worth their salt: creatures of the abyss!

When you descend to the true depths of the ocean, amid seaweed forests and coral reefs, everything seems much darker and more menacing, including the creatures you might meet.

Yet I have to be honest: some of them can actually be nice.

The trouble is that when they decide to pop up to more shallow waters (very rarely, thank goodness), they can cause disasters! For instance, some of them are so large that just by moving around, they can capsize fleets of ships without even noticing. Others cause tidal waves and hurricane-scale winds wherever they go. Then there are some . . . okay, let's just say there are some that are not nice at all and it takes very little to upset them!

Whatever happens, the important thing is to stay calm and be careful: keep working your way through this guide and you'll learn everything you need to know about creatures of the abyss . . . while having fun!

Kraken
Classification: Giant Cephalopod

Because of their enormous size, everyone thinks Krakens are always on the lookout to strike the first ship that gets in the way of their powerful tentacles.

They're not!

Krakens are very peaceful creatures that only attack when threatened. Their main problem (or, rather, the main problem for ships sailing near them) is how big Krakens are. Moving just one tentacle causes a wave so big that it's difficult even for big ships to avoid being capsized.

And as if that weren't bad enough, when Krakens lift their monstrous heads out of the water and then dive back under again, the whirlpools they produce are terrifying! More than whirlpools . . . they're like mini-tsunamis!

A Kraken's skin looks like rubber: soft and tough.

The tentacles are not only long and powerful, they have suckers along their entire length—so you certainly don't want to get hugged by a Kraken.

A Kraken's ears might be tucked out of sight, but it still hears everything happening on the surface.

Favorite Pastimes:

Krakens like rising to the surface to chill out and get some sunshine. It's a pity this is such a dangerous pastime (more for everyone else than for the Kraken): like Zaratan, Krakens are quite often mistaken for an island. To be honest, the tentacles and big, round head actually look like a small archipelago—a group of islands, in other words—and sailors are often fooled (unintentionally, of course) into thinking that they have found a safe landing spot. But when a Kraken decides to go back down below, the nightmare begins. Huge waves, dizzying whirlpools, and screams of terror!

Krakens appear in many famous novels, like Twenty Thousand Leagues Under the Sea and Moby-Dick.

What to do When you Meet a Kraken

Try to figure out whether it's awake or not. If it's napping, then slowly turn around and get away. Krakens are heavy sleepers and will take a while to wake up.

If it's already stretching out its tentacles . . . then it's every person for themselves!

They look like octopuses, even though they're often compared to giant squids (the difference is in the shape of the head: a squid's head is more pointed).

Krakens live mostly on the floor of the Norwegian Sea.

Umibozu

Classification: Humanoid

This is what usually happens: the sea will be as smooth and sheer as a mirror, there'll be a mere whisper of a breeze while everything else is silent, and into that calm the Umibozu will erupt!

Yes, literally!

Umibozus very rarely emerge from the abyss; and when they do, it's only ever at night. They prefer to be seen as little as possible. For whatever reason, Umibozus keep to themselves and want nothing to do with the other sea creatures—and less still with humans!

Their hands are almost always kept hidden underwater, yet countless sailors swear they have long tentacles instead of fingers!

An Umibozu's white eyes shine like headlamps. From the shore, they could easily be mistaken for the lights of a ship at sea.

Favorite Pastimes:

Because they're so shy, no one knows exactly what it is that Umibozus do at sea. But one thing's for sure: if they're disturbed while doing it, they hit the panic button and sink every ship in the vicinity! No escape!

As youngsters, they're cute and cuddly; but they eventually grow into veritable giants of the abyss, which is when the matter starts to get serious. Best not to get too close!

What to do When you Meet an Umibozu

When disturbed, Umibozus will ask whoever disturbed them for a large barrel. Beware, it's a trick!

On receiving the barrel (most people will hand one over right away, hoping to calm it down), the Umibozu fills it up and empties it over the sailors.

So, to be prepared in case you encounter one, keep a bottomless barrel on hand. They'll just keep trying to fill it up!

Umibozu means sea priest in Japanese (maybe because they're bald like Japanese monks).

Like Kraken, the bigger Umibozus can often wreak havoc unintentionally. Just surfacing can cause waves as high as houses!

Cadborosaurus

Classification: Sea Serpent

I call this creature *Caddy* for short, because Cadborosaurus—a name invented by scientists studying rare animals—is a bit hard to remember (and to write!).

Caddy is a spectacular creature. It's a giant sea serpent with a horse-like head and mane. And it moves just as fast (swimming, not galloping).

Its most distinctive feature is no doubt its length. There are obviously bigger creatures in the ocean's depths, but Caddy is the longest (it could even coil itself around a whale!). It has the smooth, slippery body of an eel, which makes capturing one quite tricky. You have to be careful, because once Caddy twists itself around something, there won't be much chance of escape.

The hard, pointed humps down its back remind me of a dinosaur (no, I've never actually met a dinosaur, but I've seen lots of pictures in books).

The fins might seem relatively small, but Caddy uses them to whip through the water lightning-fast!

Caddy's big eyes can see through the darkness of the watery depths.

Favorite Pastimes:

Like all serpents (sea and land), Caddy loves to coil up around something—maybe just a rock on the sea bottom, for example—although an unlucky submersible venturing too close would also be a good candidate. To have some fun, Caddy likes to pick fights with other sea monsters, tangling up a Kraken's tentacles or tickling a Namazu's whiskers (you'll soon know what that is, too!).

What to do When you Meet a Cadborosaurus

Promise me you'll try not to get trapped in its coils! Caddy is so long, it can have your feet fully immobilized in a flash (and that is trouble!).

If you want to stroke it, go ahead. It's a friendly creature. The only problem is that you'll get the back of your hand so horribly sticky that not even scrubbing with soap will get rid of it.

Captain Hagelund (a skilled fisherman) managed to capture a Caddy cub once . . . but he let it go right away, as he didn't want it to end up in an aquarium.

The first official sighting of a Caddy was in Cadboro Bay on Vancouver Island, Canada, which is where it got its name Cadborosaurus.

Namazu
Classification: Giant Fish

A Namazu is the biggest sea creature ever to have lived (bigger than anything!). Zaratan and Kraken are like goldfish in comparison.

In short, a Namazu is an enormous catfish that lives in the deepest, darkest corners of the ocean. It has been trapped under the islands and continents that have slowly formed over the millennia. So you could say it actually lives in the Earth rather than in the ocean. Truly incredible!

It's always sleepy and, luckily, rarely moves—because whenever it stretches even just a little, it causes massive earthquakes on the surface.

The most famous Namazu in the world lives deep in the earth, right under a part of Japan that regularly suffers earthquakes. The Namazu has caused, never intentionally, untold destruction.

Namazus have seven whiskers, one for each of the seven seas.

Namazus have an enormous mouth which always seems to be smiling. Do you think it is?

The movement of just one whisker can cause the earth to shake!

Favorite Pastimes:

Along with being the biggest creature of the seas, a Namazu is also the laziest. It spends a lot of time sleeping. Just as well! Like I said before, the rare times it wakes up and tries, in vain, to wriggle out of the rocks pinning it down, the devastation it causes is terrible.

Things aren't quite so bad when it merely scratches itself with one of its whiskers, just a few bigger waves than usual and the tiniest of earth tremors.

What to do When you Meet a Namazu

If you've been reading these notes attentively, you'll already know that it's impossible to meet a Namazu (they live too far below the earth). However, you might come across a namazu-e, an ancient drawing of a Namazu that took on a good-luck quality, believed to protect its keeper from nasty surprises. I made one of my own. Anyone can, to be honest. All you need is a few paints to draw a picture of a Namazu, just like the one pictured here!

According to legend, the Namazu living under Japan is pinned down by a huge stone that breaks the surface in the Kashima Temple.

Catfish are usually freshwater creatures (that is, they only live in lakes or rivers). Namazus are an exception to this rule.

Cecaelia

CLASSIFICATION: HUMAN-FISH HYBRID

This creature is like the mermaid of the abyss, except that instead of a tail for zipping through the waves, she has eight long tentacles with which she slips gracefully across the sandy sea bottom. A true lady of the ocean!

Unlike mermaids, Cecaelia is very shy and distrustful. At the first hint of danger, she sprays a cloud of black ink around her (just like the octopus and cuttlefish) and flees.

Cecaelia could actually survive out of the water, but she prefers the peace and quiet of the watery depths and would never contemplate leaving them.

She does have one thing in common, though, with her curious "cousin": Cecaelia also has a soft spot for shiny things—but she likes to swap them rather than collect them. So if you ever meet her, she might give you a precious gift (but be ready: she'll expect to receive something in return).

She prefers to wear her hair down, with no clips, and she always has a shell necklace around her neck.

Cecaelia's tentacles are not just for moving around: they're also a way of hearing what's going on nearby.

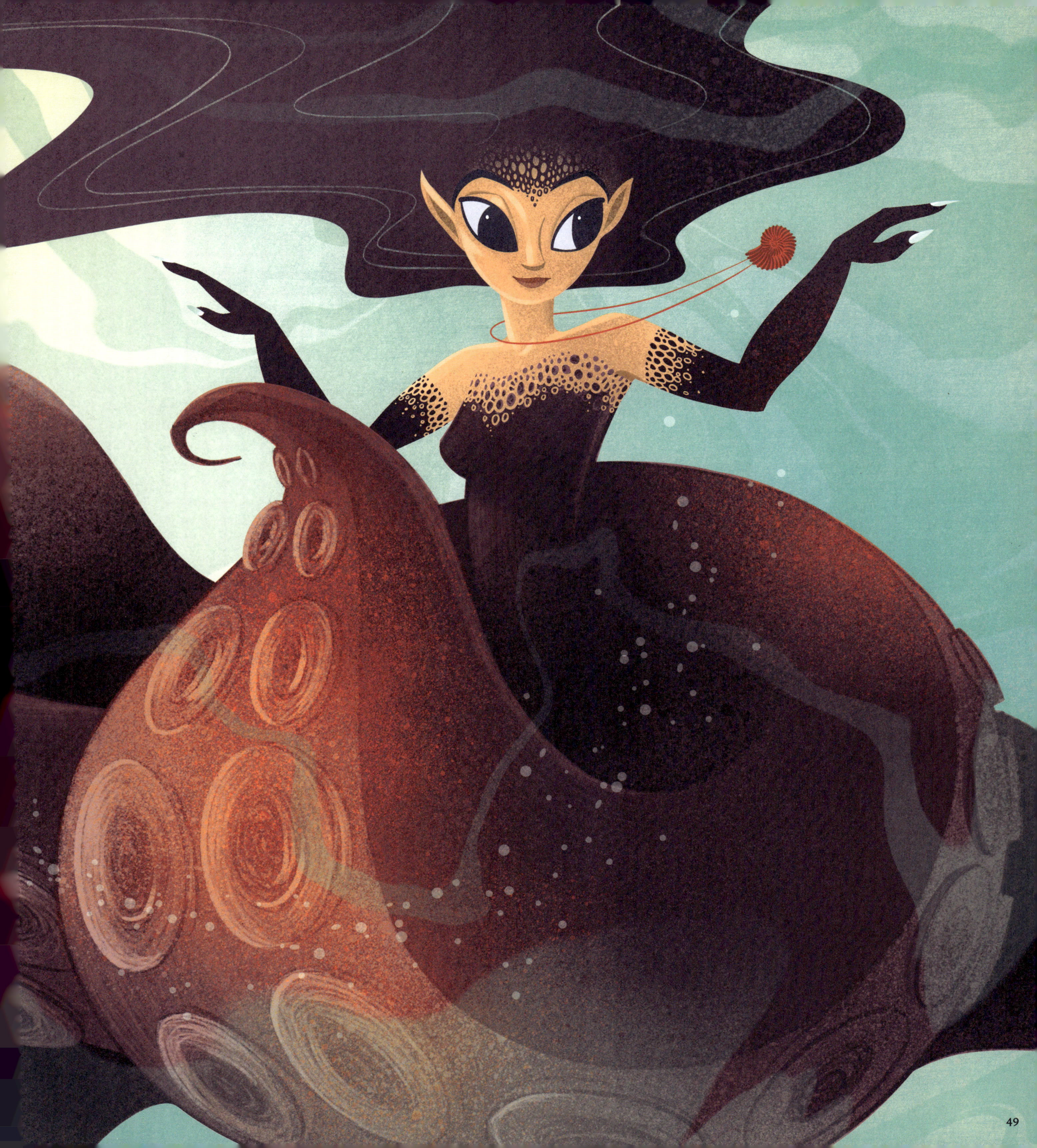

Adaro

Classification: Human-Fish Hybrid

Like Tritons (the male mermaid, remember?), Adaro is a human-fish hybrid, although it looks more like a fish than a human.

Why? Because along with the tail, it has a huge dorsal fin, like a shark, and giant gills behind its ears, which it needs to breathe while it's in the water.

What's more, where Tritons are usually relatively calm, Adaro is a malevolent beast that doesn't like humans.

It can't leave the water but, on occasion, it will travel to the land in waterspouts or along rainbows (yes, rainbows are made of water, too!).

When it gets bored, it catches as many fish as it can and throws them at fishermen (poor them!). Yes, Tritons are definitely much friendlier!

Adaro likes dressing up in bracelets and necklaces made of shells, coral, and even rusty fishing hooks.

The long horn on Adaro's forehead is like a swordfish's pointed bill.

Adaro's skin is smooth and gray, like a dolphin's.

51

Isonade
Classification: Giant Fish

Isonade is doubly dangerous because of its ability to approach people silently. Do you know what cats are like? Well, Isonade is the same, only much bigger, wetter, and with many more teeth!

Isonade makes no water jets, foamy trails, or menacing shadows. It will only make its presence felt once it's alongside its prey (which might be too late for the unsuspecting prey to escape!).

The only real clue is the wind. Sailors all agree, and I've witnessed it myself: whenever an Isonade appears, fierce winds suddenly blow. It may be a coincidence, yet it happens all the time. There's no getting away from it—Isonade is a fearsome creature. Like an enormous shark with three tails, three fins, a huge horn on its forehead, and too many (way too many) teeth!

I confess I trembled a bit, too, the first time I saw one.

Isonade's body is lined with tiny barbs, making it look like a cheese grater. Add it to your list of "animals not to stroke."

Isonade's skin is blue, another reason it's so difficult to see coming.

Cirein-Cròin
Classification: Sea Serpent

"All that glitters is not gold." My grandma likes this saying a lot, and it's also quite apt for the Cirein-cròin, although it would be more correct to say, "All that sparkles is not silver!"

This Scottish sea monster is a master of disguise, a master magician even, because it can turn itself into a small and innocent-looking silver fish. The tiniest life form, one that nobody would ever suspect!

But the real problem is that when this tiny fish lands in a fisherman's net (or if something tasty swims by), Cirein-cròin will turn back into an immense sea serpent in the blink of an eye!

And as if that weren't bad enough, Cirein-cròin is so big and its mouth so wide that it can swallow up to seven whales at once without feeling full.

So, if you ever see a Scottish fisherman bizarrely fleeing a small, defenseless-looking fish in terror, remember that he might be trying to get away from a Cirein-cròin!

The long serpent's body could capsize a ship in a flash.

When it's in its small-fish form, the silver scales sparkle in the dark.

Both the small-fish and sea-monster forms have lots of sharp teeth!

A Brief Guide to Sea Creatures

You made it! Now that you've read all my notes, sea creatures have no secrets from you. There's one more thing you need to learn, though. Something very, very important.

To be a good Guardian of Sea Creatures, not only do you need to know the difference between a cecaelia and a mermaid (do you remember?); but you also have to know the rules of the sea. Inside and out.

And know how to keep it clean.

Don't worry if you have lots of questions swirling around in your head; just read on, and all will be revealed!

The Five Golden Rules
of the Sea

① Never get too far away on your own!

When you're enjoying a swim in the sea, you can end up too far out from the shore before you realize it, which can be dangerous! Always make sure that you have an adult nearby, even if you're wearing water wings or a life vest. You never know when a Kraken might turn over in the sea, causing a high wave!

② No swimming after eating!

I know, you've probably heard it a thousand times before: swimming on a full stomach can result in a very sore stomach. And I can assure you, a stomach doing somersaults is not the best state to be in when you want to spot a sea monster! While you're waiting to digest, you could use the time to update your guardian diary.

③ Use Sun Block!

Spending hours in the sea (maybe on the trail of a Capricornus) also means spending hours under the sun at the risk of getting sunburned and going home as bright pink as a starfish (it's happened to me before, unfortunately!). To avoid this, always remember to put sun block on.

④ No throwing stones!

Skimming pebbles across the water is fun, I know (even though it's not as easy as it looks!); but when you think about it, throwing stones just for fun can be dangerous in crowded areas (and pretty stupid, if you ask me). Do you know how many mermaids have emerged from the waves with massive bumps on their heads?

⑤ Watch out for the other animals!

The sea is home to many fantastic creatures, and a lot of other species too: jellyfish that sting, crabs with sharp pincers, sea urchins with sharp spines . . . and others that simply swim about peacefully! So never let your guard down and move around carefully (you'll be a giant to some fish!).

Bluer than Blue:
Keep the Sea Clean; It's a Sea Creature's Home

The biggest danger for a marine creature is not a hunter's hook or a fisherman's net.
Far more dangerous to the sea and to those who inhabit it is pollution!
Or worse still: plastic!
Even a single plastic bottle top can cause tremendous damage. A sea creature might mistake it for food and swallow it (causing days of stomachache for sure!). And that's only the tip of the iceberg, so to speak. Environmental pollution is causing untold damage to our seas, and the consequences to our planet in general are incalculable!

So, if we want to keep our sea friends safe,
we have to learn how to look after their habitats (the places they live).

Plastic

In other words, the first thing to do is to use less plastic.
It's not difficult, really. You can small changes like not using a new plastic cup every time you have a drink, or using a glass or hard plastic one instead (the kind you can wash afterward).

An even better idea would be to carry around a cool-looking water bottle instead of a single-use plastic one.

Recycling

Another important thing to think about is separating your waste, which means throwing things into different bins: one for paper, and one for plastic and metal. That means a lot of things you throw away can be recycled. *Recycled* means turned into something else, no longer waste but something completely new. Clever magic!

On the Beach

Last but not least, **the beach needs to be kept clean as well.**

For example, don't leave trash lying around: throw it in the garbage. Maybe you can't find one? That's not a problem: just make one of your own. Put all your trash in a bag and take it home to throw away.

Because anything you leave on the beach ends up in the sea.

Don't forget. It's important!

At the Bottom of the Sea:
The Atlantis Legend

You know well now that the watery depths of our seas and oceans hide many weird and wonderful creatures, covered with fins and tentacles; but the sea has countless other mysteries to reveal to those of us brave enough to dive down to the ocean floor.
Like Atlantis, for example, the Lost City.

Some people think of Atlantis as just a city, yet legend tells us it was much, much more: an enormous, marvelous island.

Plato (one of the most important Ancient Greek philosophers) described it as having the highest towers, the most beautiful artwork, the biggest ships. . .

Apparently, the people of Atlantis were so brave and strong that they managed to conquer large swaths of land around them. Life in Atlantis flourished until they had the idea of conquering the great city of Athens. This changed everything.

Atlantis tried, failed, and then vanished into thin air. All in one day. It literally disappeared without a trace. Unbelievable, isn't it?

This happened centuries and centuries ago, but explorers and treasure hunters still scan the sea bottom to find the city. They've come across everything from tattered diving suits to the wrecks of majestic sailing ships and enormous submersibles. But there's still no sign of Atlantis itself!

What happened to Atlantis?

Maybe a Kraken did a somersault and capsized the city . . . or a Namazu finally managed to break free and set off a tsunami! Or perhaps the island was actually a Zaratan that got fed up with life on the surface. . . .

It's a mystery. Probably no one knows (although I like to imagine the many possibilities!).

Final Test
to Become a Sea Creature Guardian

I mentioned earlier that to become a full-fledged Sea Creature Guardian, you have to pass a test. That's right, the time has come (not to worry, you've made it this far, so you'll sail through it!). There's nothing too difficult, I promise, and even if you do get a question wrong, you can take the test as many times as you like, okay?

So here are the ten questions. Take a deep breath, pick up your pencil, and may the Kraken be with you!

1) What is a male mermaid called?
- A) Triton
- B) Poseidon
- C) Neptune

2) A Zaratan resembles. . .?
- A) A catfish
- B) A whale
- C) A crocodile

3) A Hippocampus does NOT have. . .?
- A) Webbed feet
- B) Hooves
- C) A mane

4) Which of these creatures has a trunk?
- A) Akhlut
- B) Makara
- C) Capricornus

5) What color is an Aughisky's coat?
- A) Black
- B) Brown
- C) White

6) Which of these creatures DOESN'T have tentacles?
- A) Kraken
- B) Cecaelia
- C) Adaro

7) The Cadborosaurus is also known as. . .?
- A) Caddy
- B) Nessie
- C) Saury

8) Which of these creatures is the biggest?
- A) Zaratan
- B) Cadborosaurus
- C) Namazu

9) How many tails does an Isonade have?
- A) 4
- B) 3
- C) 2

10) Cirein-cròin is a monster from. . .?
- A) Ireland
- B) Japan
- C) Scotland

If you Scored Five Points or Less:

I'm afraid you'll have to try again if you want to be a real Guardian!
Don't take it personally: we all get a little confused sometimes.
Flip back through my notebook, refresh your memory, then try again.
On my next trip, I bet I won't be the only
Sea Creature Guardian out at sea!

If you Scored Six Points or More:

Outstanding!
You've committed the contents of my notebook to memory. Well done!
We could do my next voyage across the seven seas together, because it's official:

You are now a full-fledged Sea Creature Guardian!

Correct answers:
1-A, 2-B, 3-B, 4-B, 5-A, 6-C, 7-A, 8-C, 9-B, 10-C

Giuseppe D'Anna

Giuseppe D'Anna was born and raised in sunny Sicily and trained to be a graphic designer and artist in the hills of Tuscany. He currently lives here and there (as well as sometimes everywhere) and occasionally has fun writing books for children and young adults.

Anna Láng

Anna Láng is a Hungarian graphic designer and illustrator who is currently living and working in Sardinia. After attending the Hungarian University of Fine Arts in Budapest, she graduated as a graphic designer in 2011. She worked for three years with an advertising agency, at the same time working with the National Theatre of Budapest. In 2013, she won the award of the city of Békéscsaba at the Hungarian Biennale of Graphic Design with her Shakespeare Poster series. At present, she is working passionately on illustrations for children's books.

White Star Kids® is a registered trademark property of White Star s.r.l.

© 2020 White Star s.r.l.
Piazzale Luigi Cadorna, 6
20123 Milan, Italy
www.whitestar.it

Translation: Denise Muir
Translation: Phillip Gaskill

All rights reserved. No part of this publication may be reproduced, stored in a retrieval system, or transmitted in any form or by any means, electronic, mechanical, photocopying, recording, or otherwise, without written permission from the publisher.

ISBN 978-88-544-1645-1
1 2 3 4 5 6   24 23 22 21 20

Printed in Italy by Rotolito S.p.A.
Seggiano di Pioltello (Milan)

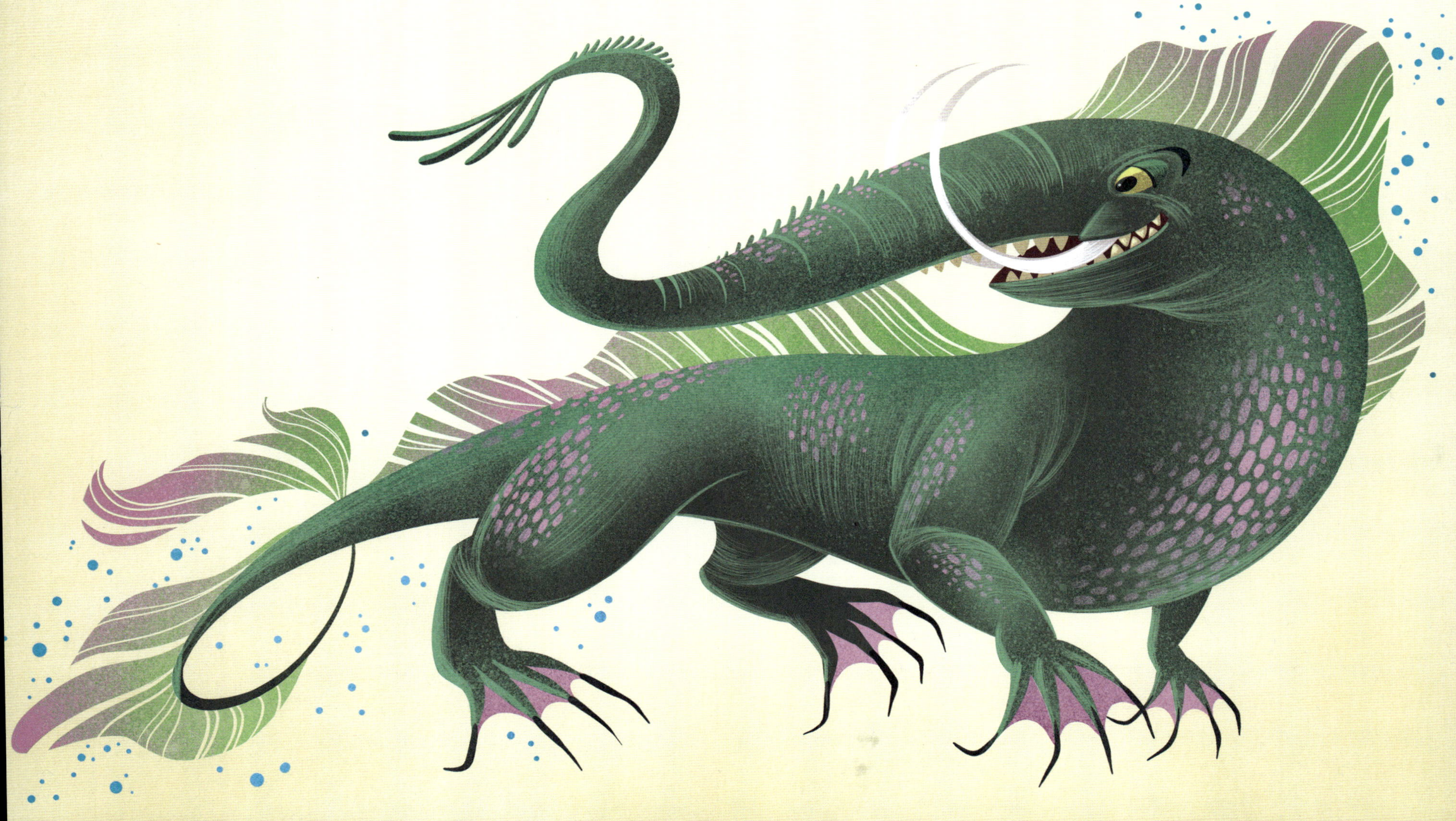

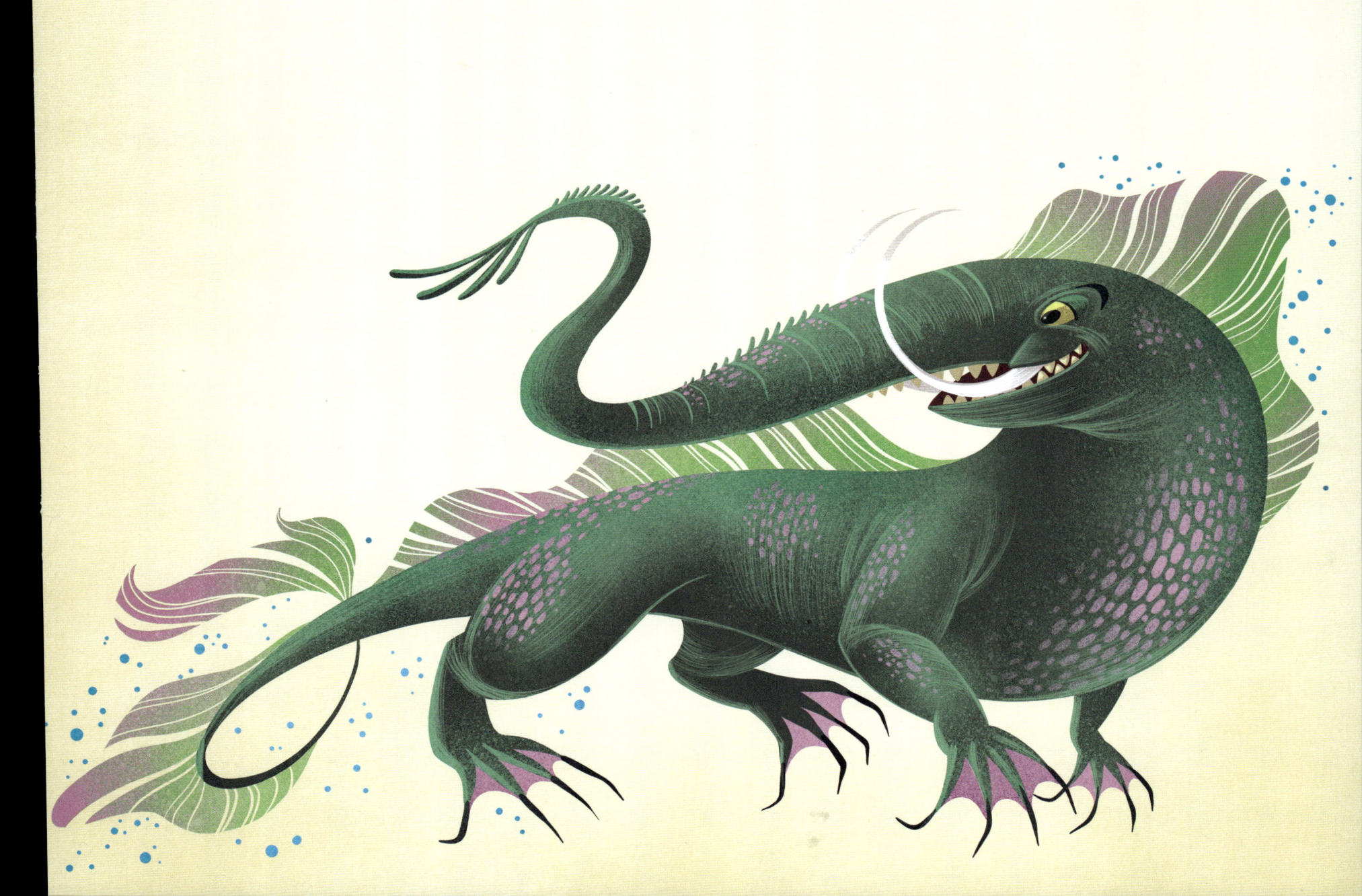